DRAWING ZENTANGLE® DECORATIONS

Jane Marbaix and Hannah Geddes

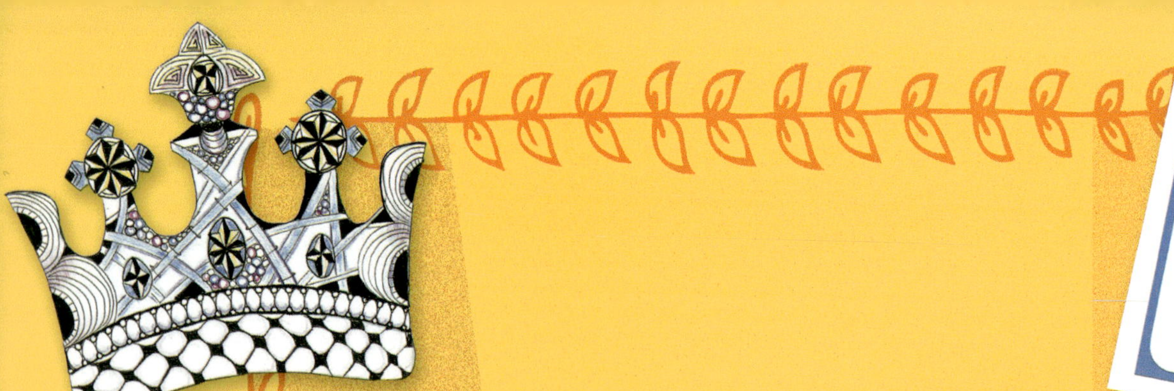

Please visit our website, www.garethstevens.com.
For a free color catalog of all our high-quality books, call toll free 1-800-542-2595 or fax 1-877-542-2596.

Cataloging-in-Publication Data

Names: Marbaix, Jane. | Geddes, Hannah.
Title: Drawing Zentangle® Decorations / Jane Marbaix and Hannah Geddes.
Description: New York : Gareth Stevens Publishing, 2020.
| Series: How to draw Zentangle® art | Includes glossary and index.
Identifiers: ISBN 9781538242674 (pbk.) | ISBN 9781538242087 (library bound)
| ISBN 9781538242681 (6 pack)
Subjects: LCSH: Decoration and ornament–Juvenile literature. | Drawing–Technique–Juvenile literature. | Repetitive patterns (Decorative arts)–Juvenile literature.
Classification: LCC TT157.M373 2019 | DDC 745.594–dc23

First Edition

Published in 2020 by
Gareth Stevens Publishing
111 East 14th Street, Suite 349
New York, NY 10003

Text, step-outs, and Zentangle Inspired Artworks: Jane Marbaix (zentanglewithjane.me)
Design: Amy McSimpson and Tokiko Morishima
Project management: Frances Evans and Katie Woolley
Outline illustrations: Katy Jackson

The Zentangle® method was created by Rick Roberts and Maria Thomas.

All the tangles in this book are Zentangle originals created by Rick Roberts and Maria Thomas, apart from: Barberpole by Suzanne McNeill (blog.suzannemcneill.com); Heartrope by Bunny Wright, Canada; Cruffle by Sandy Hunter, Texas, USA (tanglebucket.blogspot.co.uk).

Printed in the United States of America

CPSIA compliance information: Batch #CS19GS: For further information contact Gareth Stevens, New York, New York at 1-800-542-2595.

Contents

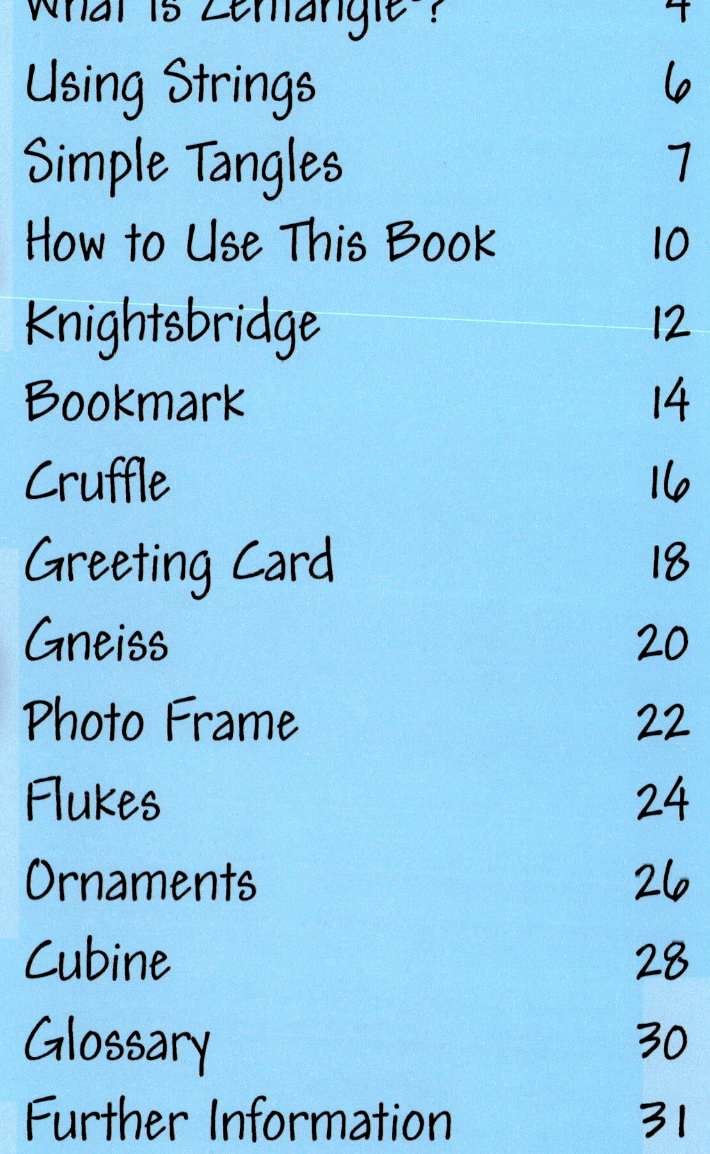

What Is Zentangle®?

Zentangle® is a drawing method created by Rick Roberts and Maria Thomas. It teaches you how to create beautiful pieces of art using simple patterns called tangles. Tangling is a fun, relaxing way to get creative, and it brings out the artist in everyone. You can tangle wherever and whenever the mood strikes you!

Getting Started

This book will show you how to draw different tangles and use them to create incredible artworks. First, find your pencils, pens, and paper, then start to create and decorate!

What you need to get started!

Pens and Pencils

You can begin making tangles with a pencil for drawing "strings" and for shading. Use a 01 (0.25 mm) black pen for fine lines, and a 08 (0.5 mm) black pen to fill in the darker areas of your pictures.

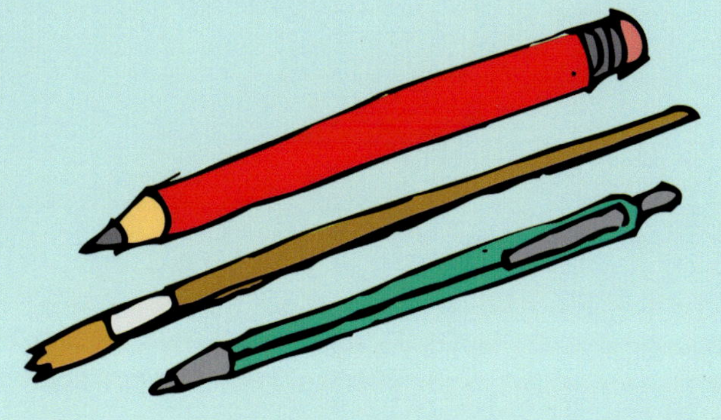

Paper

Zentangle art is usually drawn on a square 3.5-inch (9 cm) tile. Good quality artist paper or white card stock is best to use, but you can use any kind of paper. It's a good idea to also have tracing paper on hand, so you can trace images to use as outlines.

Extra Materials

Stencils are fun to use and can be found in art shops and online. Rubber stamps also make great outlines, but you'll need an inkpad to stamp them onto your paper. To brighten up your creations, you could use pens, pencils, or paints, too.

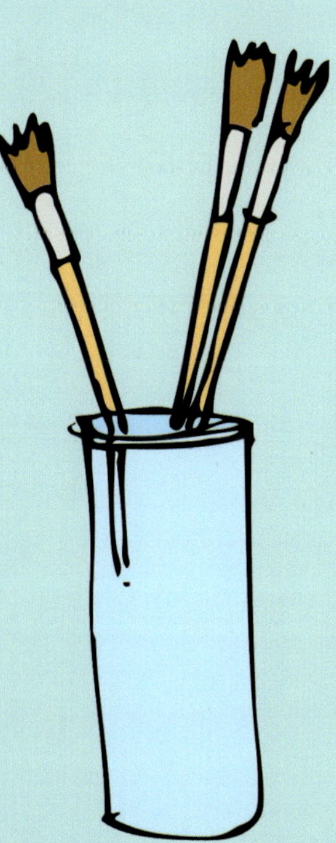

Using Strings

Strings are used to split up a large space and create smaller areas that you can tangle. They are usually drawn in pencil. We've used strings to split this square into four even triangles, but you can draw strings in any pattern you like!

1. Use a pencil to draw a dot in each corner. Join the dots together to form a square and draw two diagonal lines across it.

2. Fill the top triangle with a tangle called Printemps.

3. Then fill the right-hand triangle with Crescent Moon (page 7).

4. Fill the left-hand triangle with Hollibaugh (page 9).

5. Finally, fill the bottom triangle with Keeko (page 9).

Simple Tangles

Crescent Moon

1. Draw semicircles around the edge of your paper and shade them in.

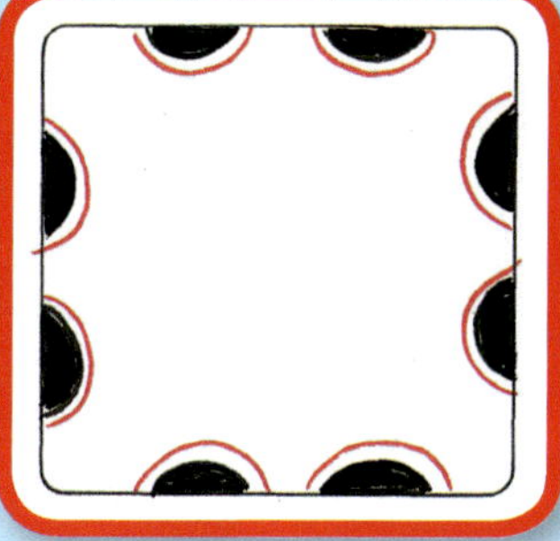

2. Draw a line around each shape.

3. Then, add some more lines around the shapes.

4. Finally, create a swirling cobweb pattern in the middle.

Tipple

1. Begin by drawing a string of circles touching one another.

2. Draw more circles of different sizes to fill the space.

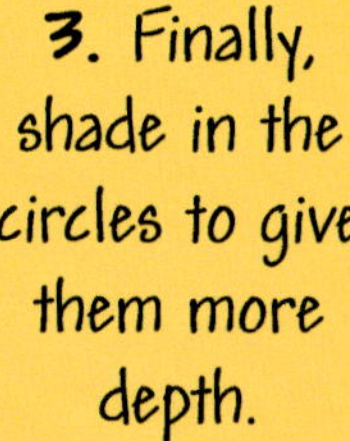

3. Finally, shade in the circles to give them more depth.

Flux

1. Draw a leaf shape.

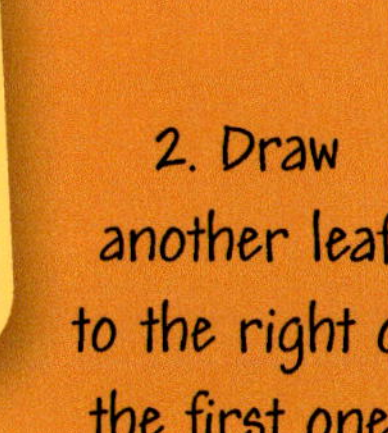

2. Draw another leaf to the right of the first one.

3. Add another leaf on top of the left-hand leaf.

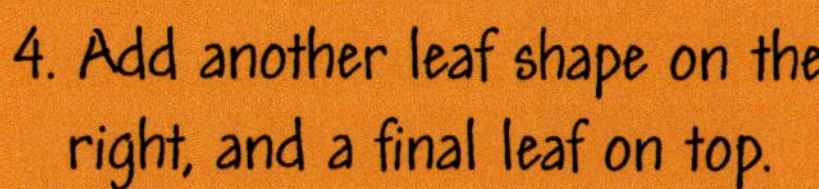

4. Add another leaf shape on the right, and a final leaf on top.

5. To finish, add some decoration to the leaves. You can draw Tipple along the bottom to create a pebbly texture.

Poke Leaf

1. Begin by drawing a stalk at the bottom of your paper. Then, draw a raindrop shape around the tip of the stalk.

2. Add more stalk and raindrop shapes to your paper.

3. Then add some shade to your tangle.

4. Add an "aura" around each leaf for a different look. You can start this tangle anywhere on your paper, like we've done, and see where it takes you!

Bales

1. Begin by drawing a grid in your space.

2. Add small oval shapes around the horizontal lines of each square in your grid.

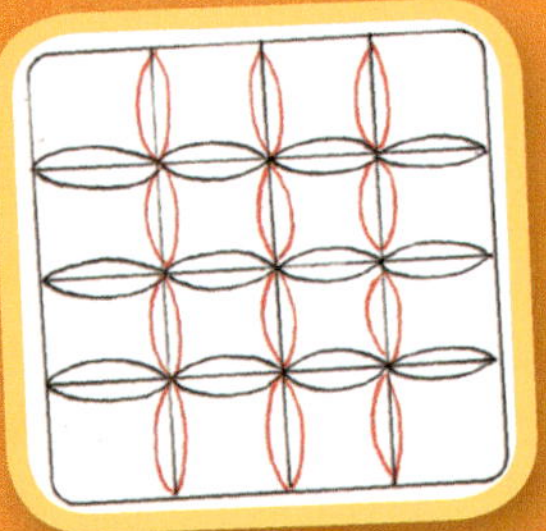

3. Then, do the same down the vertical lines.

4. Finally, add some shade to your tangle.

Mooka

1. Draw two "stems" that curve inward, following the direction of the arrows.

2. Then, with one continuous stroke, draw two more stems on your paper.

3. You will end up with this delicate tangle.

4. Finally, add some shade to your tangle for more depth.

Keeko

1. Create a cross to begin. Draw three vertical lines in the top left square, then three horizontal lines in the top right square. Do the opposite in the squares below.

2. Repeat this pattern to create a band across your paper.

3. Add another row underneath.

4. Finally, shade your tangle to give it more depth.

Florz

1. Draw three lines from the top of your paper to the bottom. Then, draw three lines from one side to the other. This makes a grid.

2. Add a diamond shape to each crossing point on your grid.

3. Finally, add some shade around the diamonds.

Hollibaugh

1. Draw a band of lines across the page.

2. Add a band going in a different direction and on either side of the original lines. This makes the second set look like they are running behind the first.

3. Then, add a small rectangle shape and some dots to the spaces between these diagonal lines.

4. Fill in the gaps between the lines with your pen, or add other tangles, such as Keeko (page 9), Printemps (page 6), and Tipple (page 7).

How to Use This Book

Now that you have practiced some tangles, it's time to get creative. You can use tangles to decorate all sorts of things, and this book will show you some great projects. A larger piece of artwork is called a Zentangle® Inspired Artwork – or ZIA. We have created some great party bunting using Zentangle® – and you can, too!

You can also buy stencils from craft stores to create ZIAs. Dreamweaver or Kala Dala stencils are really good to use.

1. Get started by cutting some white paper triangles and drawing some random strings to create separate spaces.

2. Draw a tangle in the space between each string. Then add shading to brighten your bunting.

3. Finally, make a hole in each corner of your bunting and thread them onto a string.

You will often come across these words when you tangle:

Shade This means using your pencil to darken areas of your tangle to make it POP.

Highlight These are gaps in the lines you draw in your tangles. They can make your tangle SPARKLE.

Aura If you trace around your tangle, you've added an aura. It can make your tangle come to life!

Throughout this book you'll find lots of great outlines that you can use to create your own ZIAs. Simply trace the outlines to get started with your own beautiful creations.

Knightsbridge

Knightsbridge is an easy tangle to try when you're getting started. It makes a simple grid pattern, which is perfect for this heart shape!

1. Draw wavy diagonal lines from the top corner to the opposite bottom corner. Then, draw lines in the opposite direction. This makes a grid pattern.

2. Fill in every other square in your grid.

3. Finally, add some shade to your tangle.

We've used Knightsbridge and another tangle to fill this heart shape. Why don't you trace the heart below and try yourself?

Use this outline to trace your own sweet heart shape!

The following tangles have been used in this project:

KNIGHTSBRIDGE
'Nzeppel

Bookmarks are useful to mark your place in the book you are reading and also make lovely gifts. Why not make your own, just like this one?

1. Cut out your bookmark from a piece of white paper. Then, draw some circles using a template (such as a pen cap) or a drawing compass.

2. Next, draw tangles in the circles and create a funny animal, such as a bird, or a funny face. You can join the circles using Poke Leaf, too.

3. Add black-and-white shade to your tangle for effect.

4. Finally, mount your bookmark onto red card stock and add a dash of red to finish it off!

The following tangles have been used in this project:

Printemps (page 6)
Crescent Moon (page 7)
Poke Leaf (page 8)
Tipple (page 7)
Hollibaugh (page 9)
Barberpole
Keeko (page 9)
Cruffle (page 16)
Gneiss (page 20)
Flux (page 7)

Cruffle

We love to use Cruffle when making cards and bookmarks. Follow these simple steps to create your own Cruffle tangle.

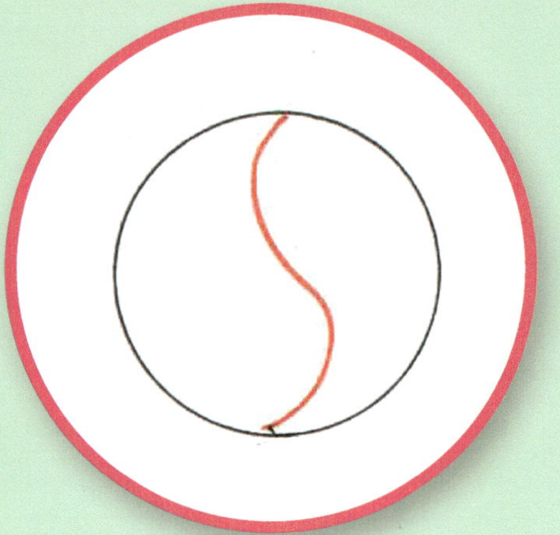

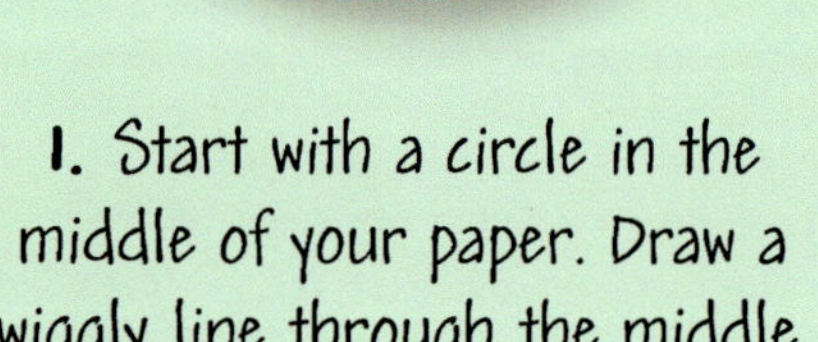

1. Start with a circle in the middle of your paper. Draw a wiggly line through the middle.

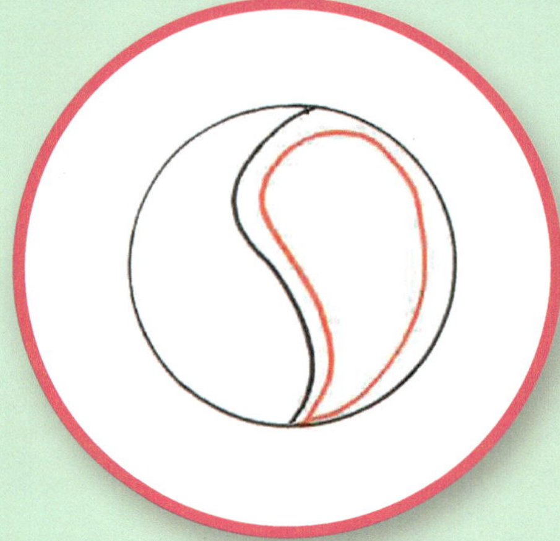

2. Draw a raindrop shape on the right-hand side, with the tip at the bottom of the circle.

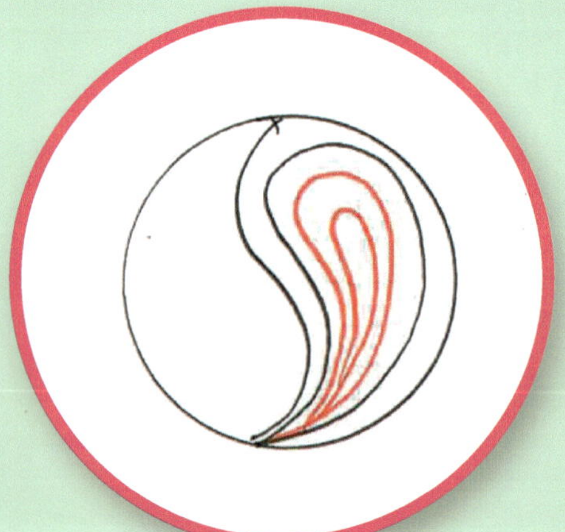

3. Fill the right-hand side with raindrop shapes that get smaller and smaller.

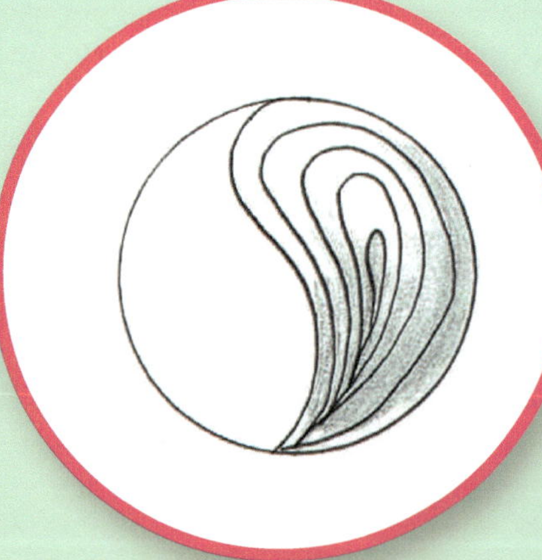

4. Add some shade to your tangle.

5. You can fill in the left-hand side, too, if you like.

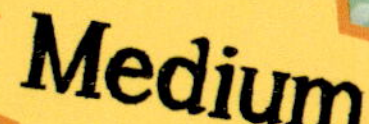

Cruffle makes a swirly tangle pattern, which is the perfect decoration for this cupcake. Why don't you give it a try?

The following tangles have been used in this project:

CRUFFLE
Hibred
Flux (page 7)

Greeting Card

It's great fun making your own greeting cards. The special someone who you send the card to will also treasure it.

1. Use your pencil to draw a pattern onto a piece of paper. We have used a Kala Dala stencil here.

2. Add tangles to the stencil. We have used Mooka (page 8) for the hearts.

3. Fill your design with any tangles you like. We've used Tipple (page 7) for the inner petals.

4. We've also added circles and tangled them with Cruffle (page 16).

Expert
The following tangles have been used in this project:
Tipple (page 7)
Cruffle (page 16)
Mooka (page 8)
5. Finally, fold a piece of card stock in half and stick your design onto the front. Your beautiful card is ready to send!
You can also use letter stencils to trace someone's name, and then tangle the name to create a personalized greeting card!

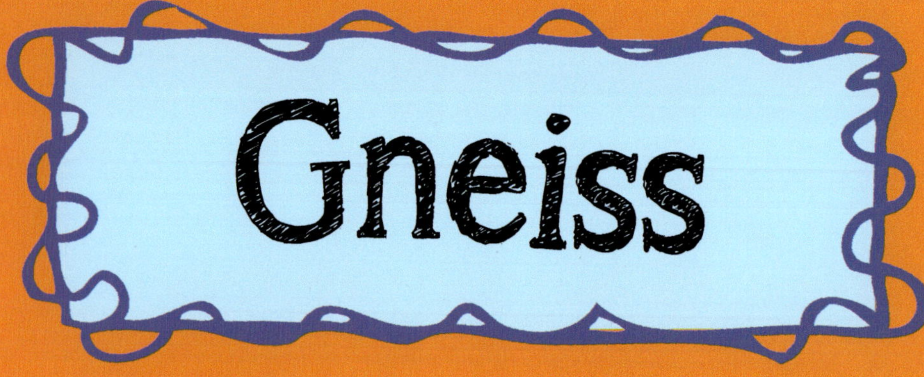

Gneiss

Gneiss creates a powerful feeling, which is perfect for this royal crown. Create your own majestic masterpiece!

1. Draw a circle and add four lines inside it, making sure they cross in the middle, like the spokes of a wheel.

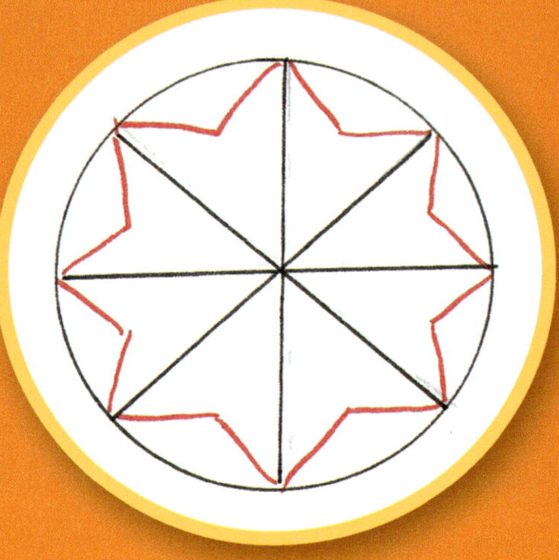

2. Next, add short, diagonal lines between the spokes, so that the shape looks like a star.

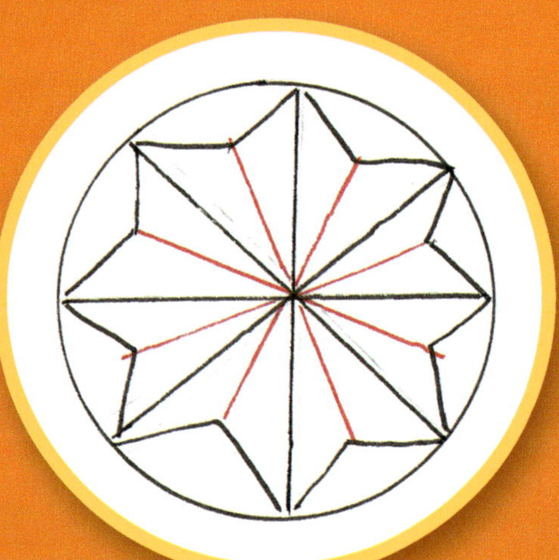

3. Draw some more lines from the middle of your star to meet the edge of your shape.

4. Shade in the left-hand side of each of the star's points.

Gneiss looks so regal! Try tangling this crown below.

The following tangles have been used in this project:

GNEISS
Crescent Moon (page 7)
Florz (page 9)
Tipple (page 7)
Hollibaugh (page 9)
Emingle
Flukes (page 24)

Photo Frame

Follow these easy steps to make your very own tangled photo frame. It's the perfect way to display a special memory.

1. Draw a frame onto a piece of white card stock, leaving enough space in the middle for your photo.

2. Make some strings within the frame. You could do straight lines or a more curved string.

3. Start to draw some tangles in the frame.

4. Then, add some shade to your tangles.

5. Finally, place your photo in the middle of your frame using tape or glue.

The following tangles have been used in this project:

Static
Crescent Moon (page 7)
Florz (page 9)
Knightsbridge (page 12)
Bales (page 8)
Poke Leaf (page 8)
Tipple (page 7)
Printemps
Hollibaugh (page 9)
Keeko (page 9)
Zander
Cubine (page 28)
Flux (page 7)
Paradox
'Nzeppel

Flukes

Flukes is an easy grid tangle to draw, but looks very impressive when it's complete. Let's give it a try!

1. Create a grid, starting at the top left-hand corner of your paper.

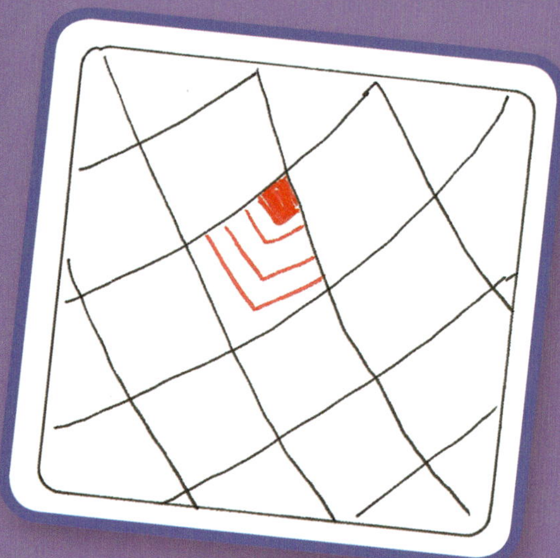

2. Draw a few "auras" inside a square. Then, shade in one corner of each square.

3. Fill all the squares on your paper with this pattern.

4. Finally, add some shade to your tangle.

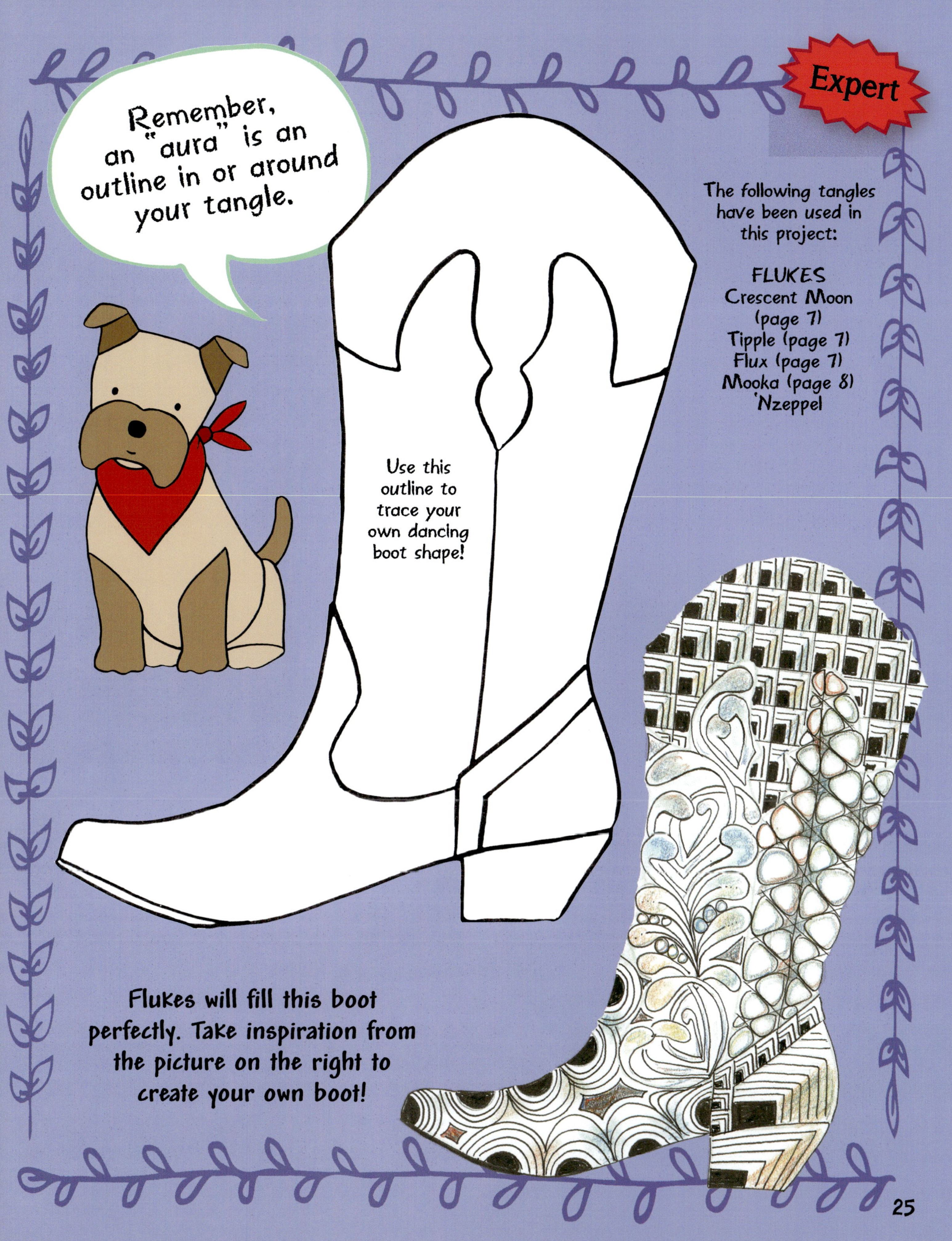
Expert
Remember, an "aura" is an outline in or around your tangle.
The following tangles have been used in this project:
FLUKES
Crescent Moon (page 7)
Tipple (page 7)
Flux (page 7)
Mooka (page 8)
'Nzeppel
Use this outline to trace your own dancing boot shape!
Flukes will fill this boot perfectly. Take inspiration from the picture on the right to create your own boot!

Ornaments

Christmas is a wonderful time of year! Add an extra bit of magic by making your own inspired decorations.

1. Take a piece of tracing paper and trace over these stencils.
2. Transfer the outlines onto a piece of thick paper and cut them out.
3. Add your strings and draw your tangles.

Use these outlines to trace your own fun ornament shapes!

Trace the lines carefully to get a smooth shape!

When you have traced these, it's time to start tangling!

This ornament shape is like a lantern!

A simple circle can be a great decoration!

4. Stick the shapes onto red and green paper for an extra festive feel. Thread a ribbon through the top and your decorations are ready to hang on the tree!

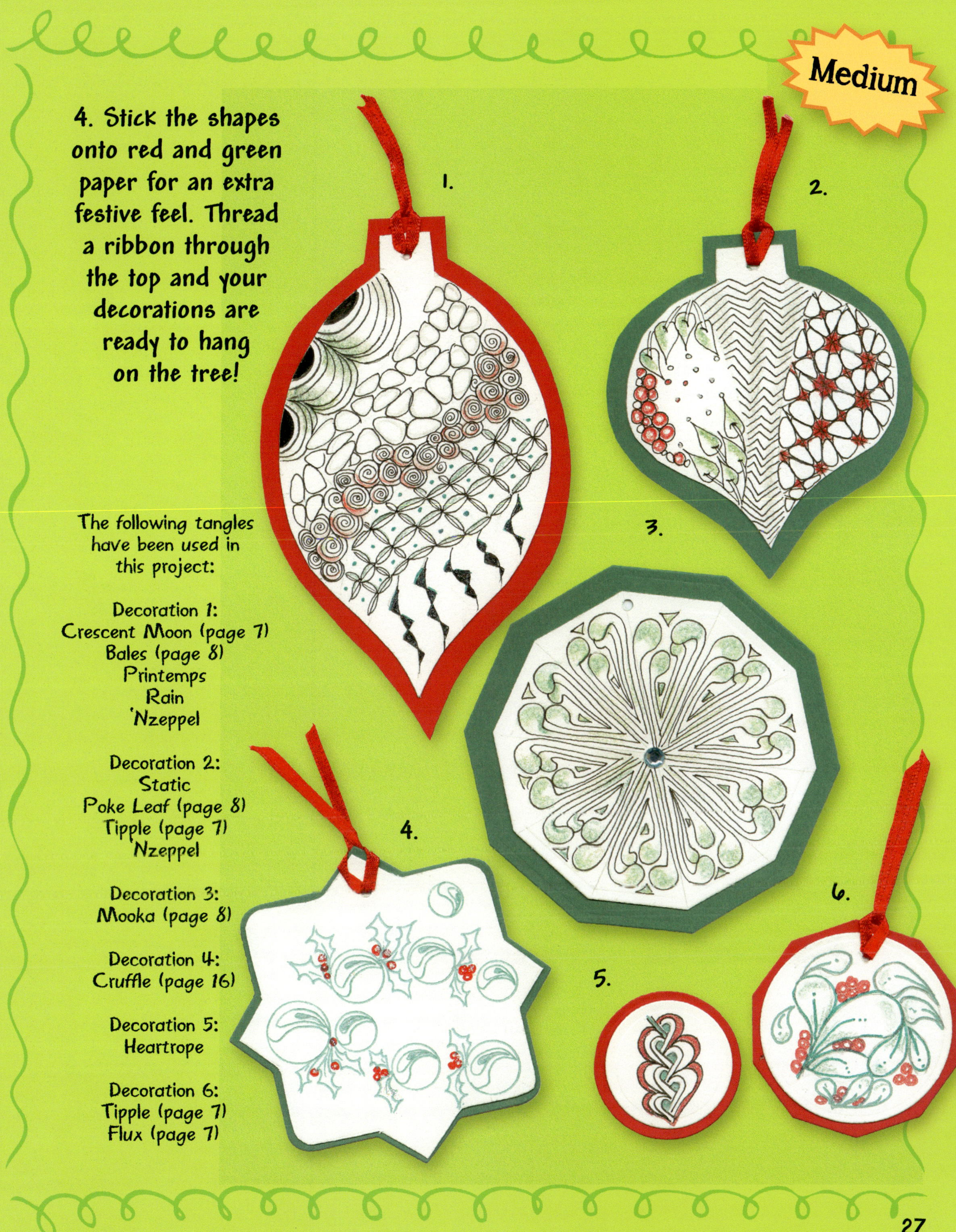

The following tangles have been used in this project:

Decoration 1:
Crescent Moon (page 7)
Bales (page 8)
Printemps
Rain
'Nzeppel

Decoration 2:
Static
Poke Leaf (page 8)
Tipple (page 7)
'Nzeppel

Decoration 3:
Mooka (page 8)

Decoration 4:
Cruffle (page 16)

Decoration 5:
Heartrope

Decoration 6:
Tipple (page 7)
Flux (page 7)

Cubine is a great tangle to use when filling large spaces in your art. Remember to take your time with each line you draw.

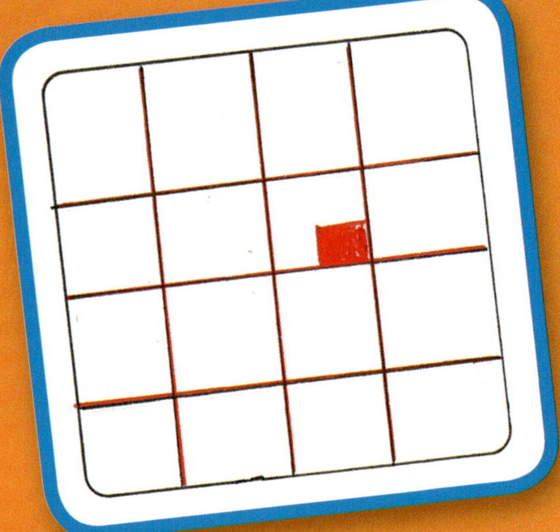

1. Begin by creating a grid to fill your space. Next, draw a small square in a corner of one of the squares in your grid.

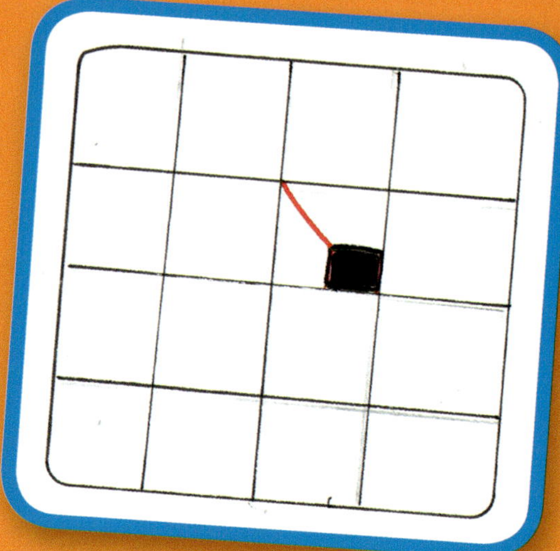

2. Draw a diagonal line reaching the opposite corner of the square.

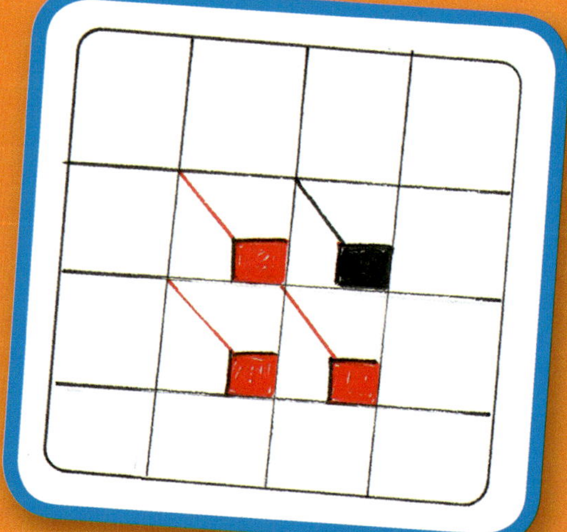

3. Continue to fill the large squares on your grid with this pattern.

4. Add shade to your tangle for depth. Fill in the rest of the grid with this pattern.

Expert
Cubine looks great in this castle picture. Its 3-D pattern really makes the towers stand out! Why don't you give it a try?
The following tangles have been used in this project:
CUBINE
Florz (page 9)
Knightsbridge (page 12)
Poke Leaf (page 8)
Flux (page 7)
Paradox
Try changing the size of your grid to create a different look!
Use this outline to trace your own fairy-tale castle shape!

Glossary

aura a line traced around the inside or outside of your tangle

diagonal a straight line at an angle

drawing compass a tool that you can use to draw circles

grid a set of horizontal and vertical lines that cross to make small squares

highlight a gap in the lines you draw in your tangles, to add a light spot

horizontal a straight line from left to right

outlines shapes with clear outlines that you can trace through another piece of paper

semicircle half a circle

spiral a shape made from a line moving outward in a circular pattern from a central point

stencil a shape that you can draw around

strings pencil lines that separate spaces on your paper

tangles a simple pattern that you repeat to fill a space

vertical a straight line from top to bottom

ZIA stands for Zentangle® Inspired Artwork

Further Information

Books

A Decorations to Cut, Stick and Fold by Fiona Watt and Amy Blay (Usborne 2014)

Flamingos, Llamas and Other Cool Things: Press Out and Decorate by Kate McLelland (Nosy Crow, 2018)

Inspiring Zentangle Projects by Jane Marbaix (Arcturus Publishing, 2016)

Let's Make Art by Susie Brooks (Wayland, 2019)

Tangled Treasures Coloring Book by Jane Monk (Creative Publishing International, 2015)

The Kids Book of Hand Lettering by Nicole Miyuki Santo (Running Kids Press, 2018)

Websites

https://zentangle.com Start by taking a look at the Zentangle® website. There's lots of information on tangles and the story of the founders of this art form.

www.funology.com Have a look at this website for craft ideas as well as recipes, trivia, and games.

www.natgeokids.com The National Geographic Kids website is packed with information about animals and amazing places.

www.pinterest.com Look up Zentangle® on Pinterest to see other people's work and ideas. (You will need to be 13 years old to open an account, or you can have a parent or teacher explore this site with you.)

www.metmuseum.org/art/online-features/metkids/ Check out the kids' section at the Metropolitan Museum of Art to find a great guide to amazing artwork.

Publisher's note to educators and parents: Our editors have carefully reviewed these websites to ensure that they are suitable for students. Many websites change frequently, however, and we cannot guarantee that a site's future contents will continue to meet our high standards of quality and educational value. Be advised that students should be closely supervised whenever they access the internet.

Index